THE ROGUE ARTIST'S WORKBOOK AND JOURNAL

WRITTEN BY RAFI

THE ROGUE ARTIST'S

LET'S GO ON AN ADVENTURE!

COPYRIGHT © 2022
The Rogue Artist's Marketing And Money Journal
By Rafi Perez

Notice of Copyright
All rights reserved by Rafi And Klee Studios. This book or any portion thereof may not be reproduced or used in any manner whatsoever without the express written permission of the publisher. Images may not be reproduced or used in any manner whatsoever without the express written permission of the contributing artists.

Edited By:
Chelsey Rhoads

Edited And Co-Authored By:
Klee Angelie Galligan

Published By:
Rafi And Klee Studios
info@rafiandklee.com

Printed in the United States of America
First Printing Edition, 2022
ISBN 978-1-7343949-7-9

HOW TO USE THE WORKBOOK AND JOURNAL

This workbook and journal has been designed to accompany the Rogue Artist's Art Marketing Guide And The Rogue Artist's Money Guide Books. It is laid out as a marketing guide workbook, to assist you in identifying your branding, mission statement, values, and come up with some of your own marketing tactics. The money section will help you come up with your weekly financial budget, figure out pricing for art, manage your money, and manage your time.

These are all methods that Klee and I use to manage our busy art career. Personally, I wanted to create something that you can refer back to and keep you on your toes. This book contains the various tools I have come up with to help me in blazing my own trail as an artist.

You can write directly in the book. I recommend not using a marker as it may bleed through. I also recommend you use it with a daily/weekly planner.

Obviously, I recommend you read "The Rogue Artist's Money Guide" and "The Rogue Artist's Art Marketing Guide" to use this book. There are certain sections that rely heavily on the content found in those books.

WHAT IS YOUR PURPOSE?

In my experience, this question can feel a little overwhelming for a creative person, especially if you just like to create stuff. It can almost feel heavy to add a purpose to something we do out of love. The thing is that "purpose" isn't supposed to be a serious affair. It is only meant for you. It is meant to assist you in getting a clear idea of what you want out of life.

Whether you are new to art or are a veteran, this is something I review periodically. Don't stress, as humans we evolve and grow and our purpose will evolve and grow with us. You can't get this wrong, it doesn't have to be altruistic, and it's not set in stone. You just want to identify where you are and what you want out of life right now. Then answer these questions and try not to overthink it.

1. **What Are You Willing to Struggle and Persist for? For how long? Why?**

2. What Did You Love Doing When You Were Young? Why?

3. If You Knew It Was Impossible To Fail, What Would You Do?

4. How Would You Want to be Remembered?

Take a deep breath, go back to the very beginning. Forget everything you think it takes to make your creative career happen. Remember and get clarity of why you exist on this planet. Think back to your childhood and remember your dreams and aspirations. If your brain starts arguing with you and telling you it's a pipe dream, tell it to go eat a bag of shirts. Then ask yourself the following questions:

1. **What is unique about you?**

2. **What unique value do you want to bring to the world?**

Next, I want you to articulate and understand your story. Understand that your story is being written right now, and the act of putting yourself out there and persisting through the suck is an epic part of your story.

Do you keep going when things get tough?

If you don't keep going and quit, what do you expect to happen?

If you keep going, or want to change that habit and keep going, why is that important to you?

The one word that can be used to describe artists who succeed at a creative career is *PERSISTENCE*. You must be persistent if you want to be able to sustain yourself with your art. Artists will have a lot of financial and emotional ups and downs. Most times, it will feel like all you have is struggle, especially in the early stages of building your creative empire. This is when your mindset has to remain optimistic and tough if you are going to work through the struggles of building a creative business that will sustain you.

Nothing in this world can take the place of persistence. Unfortunately, there are a lot of people out there who are unsuccessful and have a lot of talent. Persistence and determination are the only ingredients missing in their career.

Write your epic story of persistence. It can be a story you are currently living, or one that you want to live. What is your story?

In the beginning:

My roadblocks were:

THE ROGUE ARTIST'S

I persisted because:

JOURNAL

**I want to be remembered for bringing _____
into the world because:** **(Write a feeling here.)**

Remember, good stories connect us to our purpose and our vision. They allow us to celebrate our strengths, overcoming struggles, and creative journeys. These stories will also be the thing that connects us and our art to other humans.

IMPORTANT: You are creating your narrative. This narrative is going to be a story that shapes your opportunities. Please do not focus on what has gone or is going wrong. Focus on your overcoming, strength, and persistence. Our mind plays our narrative on repeat in the background, shaping our environment to make sense of the world. If you are focused on all the things that went wrong in the past and feel disempowered by it, your narrative is one of disempowerment. Don't ignore the struggles. The struggles are real, however you can ruminate on them or you can focus on overcoming them. Change your perspective and pivot to an empowered point of view. No matter what you may believe, you are the ONLY one who can call it quits or persist.

This is your hero's journey of how you get from there to here. Simply stated, your marketing will be a projection of that. This is how your collectors and followers will find you. They will say, "People like us do things like this." This will be your tribe and some of your most loyal supporters.

Let's write this story again as an epic adventure. On the next few pages, I want you to write your mythic story. This time we are going to write your future story as a hero's journey.

This time I really want you to lean into all the components that will help you succeed in this adventure. Patience, persistence, and maximum effort are what make an unbeatable combination for success. Most movies you love all have the hero's journey as the core of storytelling. The reason it relates to us is because ultimately, we are all on some kind of hero's journey. Let's find out what yours is.

1. The Call to Adventure

You as the hero start in the ordinary world. Suddenly something makes you decide you are going to pursue art. Why do you want to create art for a living? And how is that different from how you are living now? What is it that is calling you? It can be a suggestion from someone else or your own volition. What is the catalyst that makes you want to start your artistic journey?

2. Refusal of the Call

This may be the point in your story where you talk yourself out of it. You may refuse to pay attention to that thing that is calling you. Your reasons could be fear, indifference, insecurity, or a sense of inadequacy. Every hero refuses the call at first call. It's difficult. It takes work to push through. What were your reasons for not just going for it?

3. Supernatural Aid

This is where in most stories, a fairy godmother shows up. However, the hero's aid doesn't necessarily have to be supernatural. It can be a parent, a grandparent, a spouse, a friend, or a perfect stranger inspiring you to move forward. It is usually someone believing in you when you don't. Who is that for you in your story? Also, what miracles of coincidence helped move you along? How did persistence keep you going?

4. The Crossing of The First Threshold

This is the point where we cross the threshold. You leave the comforts and venture into the unknown world of your artistic adventure. Everything may feel like an unknown and dangerous realm where we don't know the rules and limits. It is beyond our comfort zones, and around every corner it feels like there is an unknown danger. You cross the threshold when you apply or do your first art show, approach a gallery, or put yourself out there in any way. This is when you get in the arena. How does this part of the story look like for you?

5. The Belly of the Whale

The belly of the whale represents the final separation from the world you knew. This is where you change from your old self who was too afraid to pursue their dreams, to the new version of you that is willing to do whatever it takes. This is where you are willing to undergo a metamorphosis. This is where you finally accept the call and decide to go all in. What does that look like for you?

6. The Road of Trials

This is where the crap hits the fan. The moment you accept the call, everything that you are afraid of pops out of the woods. As the hero of your story, you will face tasks and trial after trial. You will face challenges, you will be ignored, and you will feel forgotten. You may have to face them all alone. Facing these roadblocks and emotions is something you must undergo to begin the actual transformation. This is where persistence will make you stronger. The heroes keep going, the others fall into the pit of despair. What fears pop out of the woods? What goes wrong? How do you face them? How do you overcome it and keep going?

7. The Meeting with The Goddess

At this point, a small light at the end of the tunnel appears. You find a path within yourself and give up conditional validation. You realize that your journey is an adventure. Your struggles are the adventure. You become unconditional. That means that you let go of the meaning of conditions and expectations of how it should be going and realize that you are in it. What does that look like for you? How do you proceed?

8. Meeting the Temptress
This is where you as the hero will be tempted by your old life or way of thinking. This step may lead you to abandon or stray from your quest. What would that be? What would tempt or scare you to quit? How does it show itself? Do you fall for it, or keep going? Why?

9. Atonement

In this step you must confront whatever holds ultimate power in your life. It can be a person, fear, a parent, or anything that feels like it controls your emotions. This is where you embrace your growth and the sides of you that you thought were holding you back. This is where you let go of blame or guilt and move forward. What does that look like for you?

10. Apotheosis

Now that you have let go of fear, you feel unstoppable. You are putting yourself out there boldly and people identify with you and your art. However, this is your biggest obstacle. It is your biggest challenge. You are at the threshold and everyone is rooting for you. However, you don't know if you have it in you. This is the highest point in the development of your creative journey. This feels like the culmination or climax of the adventure. What does this look like for you? How do you face it?

11. The Ultimate Boon

The ultimate boon is the achievement of your goal. This is what you were after and why you took the journey to begin with. You have conquered your deepest fears, insecurities, and beliefs that held you back in the first place. You won the battle with stage fright. You won the battle against the fear that you and your art are not good enough. However, now you have new fears, and new goals. And although you feel that you can confront anything that is thrown at you, the obstacles will still be challenging. What does that look like? Where do you go from here? How does it feel? Do you persist? Why?

You may think this is the end of the story, but the interesting thing about life is that the story continues. This is now your new normal, and the next part of the adventure will take you through other unknown lands and many more challenges. In every adventure, you will find that you must reach inside to discover your inner power. Everything is an inside job. Everything is an emotional story.

This is the point where I've had artists angrily exclaim that they don't have a story. However, you do have a story, and it is still in the making. The simple act of putting yourself out there becomes a significant plot point in your narrative. When you go out there and face rejection, fear, being ignored, criticism, and keep going despite all of that, your tale becomes an epic saga.

Imagine for a moment if Dali, Picasso, Banksy, or Warhol quit when they ran into their first or second roadblock. Every one of these artists were ignored for a vast portion of their life, yet never settled for living a life where they faced no obstacles. What if they traded in their paint supplies for a stable job and security? What if they didn't push the envelope and themselves through the financially rough times? What if they quit? There would be no story.

Be Yourself. Be Real. Be Personal.

Your story may not feel like it is compelling, but it's not over. When you put yourself out there, the elements in life that put you where you are now will play a significant part of that narrative. However, every good epic needs hardship and growth. So when we embark on our journey to put ourselves out there, we create our own compelling story. Our novel is less of a hero's journey if we avoid rejection, fear, being ignored, criticism, and pain.

MISSION STATEMENT AND GUIDING PRINCIPLES

Your mission statement should reflect your unique approach to art and the world. To come up with one that incorporates all the significant components of your art career, start with these questions.

1. Why do you create what you create? Think about the spark that ignited your drive to create. What will keep it lit?

THE ROGUE ARTIST'S

2. Who are your collectors? What can your creations do for them? How will it enrich their lives now and in the future?

3. What image do you want to convey? How do you want people to think of you?

4. What is the nature of what you create? How does this relate to your message? How might this change over time?

5. What experience will your audience be left with? Define what makes your interaction so extraordinary.

6. How do you plan to challenge yourself? What are the fears you plan to tackle in putting yourself out there?

7. What kind of relationships will you maintain with your audience? Every artist is in partnership with collectors who invest in them. When you succeed, so do they.

8. What sets you apart? What is uniquely you? Is it your art? Your style? Your sense of humor? Your perspective? What are your strengths?

9. How will you put yourself out there? Describe your strategy and how you plan on staying authentic.

10. What underlying philosophy guided your responses to the previous questions? This will clarify the "why" behind your mission.

Ok, now that you have had time to think and write about what you are about. Let's create your mission and values statement.

What is your mission?
Come up with a sentence that explains what you are about and what you want to bring to the world.

Then list your values. Come up with sentences that describe how you will interact with other people and why. I started some sentences so you can work it out on the next few pages. Also, if you get stuck, I listed our mission and value statement at the end of this exercise. Please try to create your own before you look at any other examples of a mission statement.

To point the lens on how:

To share what I've learned to help:

To create a culture of:

To treat myself and others with:

To have the courage to:

To not chase:

To approach every personal or career challenge as a:

To challenge the status quo and nurture a community of:

To remain:

To keep _____ in mind when I:

And finally, how will you put this message out there and share it with the world authentically?

Ok, so now, take all of that and write down your new mission statement and values. Remember, this isn't the end all be all, chances are this will evolve and change throughout your career.

What is your Mission Statement? Keep it short and sweet.

What are your guiding principles or values? These are the things you keep in mind when making choices.

Continued

Your Mission Statement gives you excellent footing in who you are and gives you the confidence to stop chasing validation or permission to be you. When you put yourself out there, it will make things much easier for you in communicating who you are and what you stand for if you know more about who you are.

Rafi & Klee's MISSION
To inspire and encourage creativity and empowerment in the human spirit with everything we create and do.

Rafi & Klee's VALUES
We live these values in everything we put out there and everything we do:

- To point the lens on how beautiful and powerful a single human being is and how they can influence the world.
- To share what we've learned to help artists and humans who may be curious, and do it freely and openly.
- To create a culture of creativity, laughter, empowerment, and innovation where everyone is welcome.
- To treat ourselves and others with humanity, love, understanding, and patience in everything we do.
- To have the courage to say no when something doesn't fit our values, but without arrogance or hubris.
- To not chase money, fame, likes, subscribers, accolades, power, or validation as a definition of success.
- To approach every personal or career challenge as an opportunity to grow and act with courage.
- To challenge the status quo and nurture a community without hierarchy – seeing EVERYONE as equal.
- To remain real, connecting with transparency, authenticity, empathy, and respect for all in everything we create.
- To keep ethics, sustainability, and the environment in mind in the choices we make for our business.

These are questions we ask ourselves when doing anything out in the world. These are based on our mission and values. Think about who you are and what you do. See if you can question your deeper motives. This is a great exercise for when you want to make sure you are staying true to yourself. Really think about these for a moment and go deep if you have to. It is vital to know what motivates your decisions. These questions can be used to look at your overarching motives, or a single decision you might be facing.

If you knew that someone could not do a single thing for you, would you treat them differently than someone you could get something from?

Do you feel empowered by doing this, or are you doing it out of fear, desperation, spite, or validation?
(Empowerment is about ways of thinking and supporting yourself to feel in control and responsible for your own life and emotions.) If you are blaming, excusing, or needing to impress someone else, then rethink your motives.

Am I doing this because I feel that I am entitled? Is it a choice based on someone else's entitlement?

Am I doing this because I feel that I owe them? Am I doing this because I feel that they owe me?

Am I doing this because I feel that I need them? Am I doing this because I feel that they need me?

How will this *Actually* benefit the world?
Any time you share anything in the world, there should be a benefit for others. Whether you inspire them, make them smile, think, or feel – then it is powerful. If you are just saying "Hey look at me!" then rethink your motives.

JOURNAL

CREATE YOUR AVATAR OR ACTION FIGURE

Now that you know your story, mission, and values, let's come up with your avatar or action figure. This is what your branding is going to look like. Everything you do is part of your brand, that is because YOU are your brand.

Let's have fun designing the packaging and display for who you are. Pull out your colored pencils and your creativity and let's design your brand identity. Sketch a box that will house your action figure that represents you after answering a few questions.

If you need help with this, open up The Rogue Artist's Art Marketing Guidebook, and go to the ADD SOME ROGUE WITH SOME ROUGE section for color meanings. Also look at THE POWER OF WORDS section for what you write on your box.

What is the name on the box?

What is the mood of the message in color and word?

What does the logo look like?

What colors are on the box?

What color are the fonts?

What kind of font are you using?

What is the purpose of your character?

What promise does your character stand by?

What is your character's personality?

What scene is around your character?

What description is on the box?

Are there any warning labels?

How is the character dressed?

Are there any accessories?

Ok, now that you have identified what the components look like, it is time to draw it out on the next few pages.

Just like your personal identity makes you uniquely you, your brand identity is the special sauce of your creative business that sets you apart from every other brand out there. The key is to have fun with this and make sure it represents what you are all about.

THE ROGUE ARTIST'S

DESIGN AVATAR

DESIGN AVATAR

THE ROGUE ARTIST'S

DESIGN AVATAR

DESIGN AVATAR

THE ROGUE ARTIST'S

Now comes a little more fun. We are going to come up with an awesome tagline for your character. My rule of thumb is to keep your **tagline** simple. Too many slogans out there try to say too much. You should explain what you are about in two to ten words. Think of it as your brand motto. A motto isn't just about marketing. It's about letting people know what you are all about.

Think about words that you really like, words that evoke a feeling in you and align with what you are all about. You might start by just listing words that have potential, then try arranging them in different ways until they say something that really speaks to you.

This is your creative motto.

> Our creative motto is "Inspired By The Stuff Of Life."
> Our audio tagline is "Total Awesomeness!"
> My tagline for my artwork is "Dynamic Depictions Of The Human Experience."
> Klee's jewelry tagline is "Inherently Lovely."

You want it to be short, sweet, and represent you in two to ten words. The shorter the better. Other taglines include: Got Milk? - Just Do It. - I'm Lovin' It. - Maybe she's born with it. Maybe it's Maybelline. People might share your tagline on social media if they find it funny, memorable, or both.

Use the space below to capture who you are and what you want to put out there in 2 - 10 words. Then put this on everything you share so people become familiar with it. Take your time with this and have fun.

1) Write a paragraph that explains who you are, what you do, and what you are all about.

Make it a brain dump. Allow yourself to write down all the things that pop into your head.

2) Condense that paragraph down to one line or two.
Try to get to the core of what you are trying to say. Have fun with this and see how many two liners you can come up with.

3) Condense it down even more.
Ok, here's the REALLY fun part. Now it's time to tighten and polish this down to one line. Come up with some one-liners.

4) Test your taglines on unsuspecting bystanders.
Let people know what your new awesome tagline is. Pay attention to how people respond, what associations they make to it, and most importantly how you feel saying it.

If it doesn't make you feel like a badass, or people don't get it, just continue tweaking it until you have something you feel good about. You want to be proud of your tagline and feel like it represents you.

Draw a picture of your tagline below and add some flourishes for your branding.

Now that you have your story, mission, values, brand image, and tagline, I want you to have fun with it. This is the first leg of putting yourself out there and it is going to happen in your imagination. I want you to write down your ideas and most definitely have fun with this.

What does your TV ad look and sound like?

What about your radio ad – what does it sound like, what are they saying?

Sketch out your magazine ad.

THE ROGUE ARTIST'S

Sketch out your outdoor ads and posters.

What does the website look and sound like?

PUTTING YOURSELF OUT THERE ONLINE

When it comes to putting yourself out there online (whether you are using social media, your blog, paying for ads, or anything), it's important to ask yourself a few questions to really give you direction. Turn your marketing itself into something that benefits and entertains people whether they purchase or not. Think of everything you put out there as an opportunity to share part of your story. One of the biggest problems I see with artists who have a hard time growing a following online is that what they share is boring.

I hate to break it to you, but sharing a picture of your art with a quick price and title is boring. No one cares. Here are a few questions you can ask yourself about what you share.

Is what I'm doing interesting?
If you don't find it interesting, then nobody else will.

Am I creating something extraordinary out there that people might talk about?

When I post, am I just going through the motions sharing my story?

Is what I'm doing inspiring?

Am I creating an unforgettable experience?
Anything I put out in the world is marketing, so my marketing should be fantastic. Whatever I put out there I ask, "Is it capturing or creating a memorable moment? Or is it just a throwaway post, event, or ad?"

JOURNAL

Go on one of your social media pages and pick out one of your posts. Go ahead and do that now, I'll wait. Take a good look at it and then look at the next one. Ask yourself these questions. Jot down your answers so you can keep a record of what may need to change.

Does this post say anything about me? If not, how can I change that in the future?

Does this post make me look like I'm just desperate to sell my art? Am I giving them anything other than the "buy this" vibe?

Will this post inspire anyone? Does this post inspire me? What value is it bringing in of itself?

Does this post represent who I am and what I'm about? If not, what can I change?

What story will future generations tell about me based on this post? Will they have *ANYTHING* interesting to say?

Am I actually trying to connect with people or am I avoiding the connection by being aloof?

Do I enjoy looking back at my own posts? Are they captivating to me?

What can I do to make what I share more compelling?

JOURNAL

What is the theme that I see when I put all my social media posts together? Is it one big lame blur or is it a compelling story?

How can I make it compelling? Are my pictures and words telling a story? Would I feel like I know "Me" if I came across my posts?

IN PERSON ROGUE CHECKLIST

Ok, so now you have a better understanding of why what you share online is compelling or not. Apply these questions to EVERYTHING you share online. Posts, blogs, newsletters, ads, videos, podcasts, pages on your website, and everything else you share can be compelling and offer value.

However, sharing online is just a part of putting yourself out there. Honestly, the biggest challenge will be facing the world in person. This is a challenge that will help you grow through your insecurity much faster than online. Look at the challenges I have listed and check off the ones you have done. If any of these cause you to flee in terror, then you know it is a comfort zone you may want to face. I recommend doing everything on this list at least once.

Many artists will contact me and think there is some secret to marketing and I will always disappoint them. The truth is that there is no easy way around it. You must get out there and face challenges. You must get in the arena and put yourself in the crosshairs of rejection, criticism, public failure, and falling on your face.

I find it interesting that when I talk about rejection, some artists will respond by saying, "I wish I was being rejected, at least that way someone is showing *SOME* interest." They will usually say this because they have no traction on social media or something like that.

The reality is that if you are not being rejected, it is because you are being safe and not taking any risks. Sure you are posting on social media, but are you REALLY putting yourself out there and taking risks?

The worst thing that will happen online is that you will be ignored because you are not reaching anyone. There's no risk in that. Honestly, it is sharing your real-life experiences that will help you connect. So, get out there.

JOURNAL

- ◯ Register your business at your county office.
- ◯ Contact local farmers markets and see if they accept art.
- ◯ Contact local galleries and see how to apply.
- ◯ Start a website and write blogs.
- ◯ Sign up for local art shows in your area.
- ◯ Sign up for small art walk events.
- ◯ Go to art shows and ask artists which art shows they recommend.
- ◯ Contact events where your art might be a good fit.
- ◯ Contact local businesses where your art might be a good fit.
- ◯ Enter local art competitions and open calls at galleries.
- ◯ Do some outdoor painting, creating, or music at a public location.
- ◯ Hand out 100 business cards in a day.
- ◯ Join art groups or attend art meetings in your area.
- ◯ Travel to art festivals.
- ◯ Create videos of you creating and share them online.
- ◯ Get permission to do a free live painting or demo at a public event.
- ◯ Hang something fun on community bulletin boards.
- ◯ Hang up fun street banners or posters.
- ◯ Do a mini-art scavenger hunt.
- ◯ Do an open studio.
- ◯ Hold an online virtual art tour, concert, or show.
- ◯ Create a catalog of your art and leave them with local businesses.
- ◯ Take some chalk out on the town and leave inspiring messages.
- ◯ Do an artist talk at a school or group.
- ◯ Release a book or booklet of something fun about your art.
- ◯ Partner with a local business for an art show.
- ◯ Talk about your art to strangers.
- ◯ Get a credit card reader so you can accept credit cards.
- ◯ Learn about digital payment methods so you keep up to date.
- ◯ Work on a public mural or get involved in a community art project.
- ◯ Do a free live webinar or live event of you creating.
- ◯ Teach a creative workshop.
- ◯ Collaborate with other artists in the area on how to market each other.
- ◯ Attend art events in your community and introduce yourself.

BRAINSTORM HOW AND WHY TO PUT IT OUT THERE

Brainstorm some fun outlandish ideas that fit your art and personality. For example, one of my future plans is to create a small treasure hunt booklet with my art, puzzles, riddles, and cyphers that reveal the location across three states of buried treasure. This would be a huge marketing campaign and may get some national attention if I do it right. I'm still in the preparation stage but feel free to steal it if you wish, I'm stealing it from someone else. The larger the project the better. Make it fun and something you would enjoy putting out there.

What am I promoting?

What series, message, or part of your creative business are you promoting? For example, we promote our music slightly differently than we do art. I also promote my abstracts differently than I do my portraits. List all the different things you want to promote. It could also be your message or what you want to share.

How will these things individually benefit people?

Who are these for? Who would these appeal to?

For example if you do pet portraits, it will appeal to pet owners. If you do empowering art, it will appeal to people who are looking to feel empowered. If you create feel good music, it will appeal to people who want to feel good. Try to think of the answer in emotional terms.

Can my art or message bring someone emotional satisfaction or relief? Take a look at THE COMPELLING NEED TO BUY ART chapter in The Rogue Artist's Art marketing book for some guidance here.

Why am I sharing this? Be honest with yourself because your underlying motivations will always shine through.

Why would *MY* followers care about this?

Where could I share this?
List where and how you could share this out there and why you think it would be received well.

Why now?
Is there a reason you are choosing to share it now? Does timing matter?

Will the way I share it be exciting and creative?
Is this something you are genuinely excited about? Will you spread mutual excitement with how you put it out there?

How can I improve on this idea?
Am I thinking outside of the box and having fun brainstorming this? If not, **How can I make it more exciting?**

(Continued)

GUIDELINES TO FOLLOW

Belief. If you believe in the art you make, then you have a story worth telling. You are making a contribution worth talking about. There is no need to persuade someone to buy when you believe in what you are doing and why. They will connect with you on a deeper level than any deceptive marketing tactics can achieve.

Why do you believe in your art and what you are trying to say?

Meaningful Connections. Build, design, and create something that means something to you. Your masterpiece or opus is your life. It's not about getting mass media to like you. It's about connecting with a few like-minded people who will benefit and care. They will find you little by little. There are billions of people on the planet. Just a tiny fraction of that is more connection than you will ever need.

How can I create a meaningful connection?

Be Authentic. You are not competing with anyone else. You are simply allowing like-minded people to find you. Your story will match the narrative of your people, be honest about your intentions, and build trust. In doing this, you become your own trusted brand. When this happens, more people will find you. Say what you mean, and mean what you say.

Am I being real in the way I put myself out in the world? How am I using my voice?

Mutual Excitement. In one simple word, marketing is all about word of mouth. On the internet, things go viral because people are sharing them. It is like digital word of mouth. You don't have to cause controversy or be edgy to get people talking. Excitement is contagious, be authentically excited about what you are up to.

Are you excited about what you are sharing? Do you show it?

Be Human. People who buy your creations are intelligent and beautiful human beings. Do not allow yourself to fall into the "Me Vs. Them" trap, and don't look at people like wallets with legs. You cannot connect with people if you dehumanize them. Most people approach marketing from a selfish perspective, "What can I get from the consumer?" vs. "What can I give?" Be giving and act with humanity. That will set you apart from the norm.

What is my perspective on this? Do I give or do I try to take? Do I view the world as difficult?

Be Persistent. Show up every day even if no one else comes to the party. Remain generous and enthusiastic about what you are doing for the rest of your artistic journey. Keep producing art, keep putting yourself out there, and keep striving to be genuine. Allow people time to build a relationship with you and what you are doing. Earn trust, don't assume you are entitled, and understand that trust takes time.

Am I willing to go all the way and persist through all the roadblocks?

Be Flexible. Change things up, pivot, and change direction if you have to. Try not to be rigid in your approach to putting yourself out there. Be willing to try new things and take chances. Do incredible things and think outside of the box. If things aren't working, change it up and take a new approach. If they are working, don't coast. Always be experimenting and playing around with new ways of putting yourself out there. Most importantly, don't quit. Just change it up.

Am I rigid in my approach or do I have the ability to be flexible? Investigate this.

PAYING FOR ADS

If you are going to pay for an ad, make sure you set yourself apart from the typical boring ads that are out there. Ask yourself these questions to determine whether it is worth it.

What can you do differently with your ad to make it fun?

What would make your ad awesome?

Will people share your ad? Why?

What benefit does the ad provide the person watching in itself?

THE ROGUE ARTIST'S

What can you learn from putting this ad out there?

Will people talk about this ad at lunch?

Are you so proud of the ad that you consider it art? Why?

A lot of ads are just based on "Hey look at me and buy my stuff!" You want to give people a benefit. I think it is rude to interrupt someone's life experience with a desperate plea to spend their money on your stuff. I want people to think of me and smile. I like the words authentic, fun, meaningful, and valuable to be what comes to mind when people think of me and my art. I don't want them to sigh and skip my ad.

PUTTING YOURSELF OUT THERE TO DO LIST

Write down all the fun and exciting ways you want to challenge yourself to put yourself out there this year. Think outside the box. Make this a brain dump and just go for it. Add ideas on the next several pages.

PUT YOURSELF OUT THERE LIST

PUT YOURSELF OUT THERE LIST

MORE BRAINSTORMING

Here is a list of ideas for putting yourself out there. Take these and role with them or come up with your own. Conduct an art social experiment to see how people respond to your style of marketing.

- **Show It Off.** Put a piece of art on the outside of your car and let the world know you are an artist.
- Come up with a **CRAZY ELEVATOR PITCH** and tell at least 5 random people that day.
- **Put Them Around Town.** Make large and/or tiny outside art signs that make people stop.
- **Have An Art Scavenger Hunt** where you leave at least 30 to 42 pieces around a town.
- **Create A Coloring Book Flier** or poster with a crayon attached.
- **Put Together A Rogue Street Team**. Have fun coming up with elaborate plans and missions. Like flip signs in unison.
- **Give Away 100 Business Cards** in 3 hours.
- **Don't Take No.** Go to ALL the local businesses and ask if you can display your art there. Don't stop until you've been rejected 25 times.
- **Remember Your Loyal Collectors.** Send a special handmade card. Just to let them know they are even more special.
- **Set Up A Yard N Art Show.** Or better yet: A Neighborhood group art show.
- **Grab Some Chalk** and create some art outside.
- **Introduce Yourself** As your Social Media Handle for a week… In person and online.
- **Go To A Public Place**, like a park or something and paint, sketch, dance, or practice music.
- **Have A Random Acts Of Art Week** where you go out and personally give someone some art, just because you want to brighten their day.
- **Hide One Piece Of Art Somewhere** And post five riddles that need to be solved in order to find it.

- **Do A Mural** for a local business and work on it during the busiest times.
- **Give Random Objects Around Town A Personality** with construction paper and googly eyes and sign with your hashtag.
- **Leave About 100 Positive Messages** around town with homemade magnets. Something that will make people smile.
- **Whenever You Are Waiting In Line** sketch something on some random item or scratch paper, sign it, add your website, and leave it there.
- **Host A Live Painting** event with a local business, or at a party.
- **Host An Art Party** event where people can dress up as their favorite artists or characters.
- **Host Your Own Big Artworld Style Auction** with paddles and fancy clothing, just less expensive and more fun.
- **Create An Interactive Piece Of Art** and sit at a park and challenge people to use it.
- **Online - Create An Anti-Ad Campaign** that highlights your sense of humor... we all have one... hopefully.
- **Online - Have A Virtual Open Studio** and let people hangout with you while you create.

Don't stick to the traditional options to spread the word of what you are doing. The more harebrained the better. Our art brings us a sense of creative joy, just spread that with everything you do.

Use your creativity to expand your reach. It is unmatched. Do you think Banksy became popular by buying ads on Facebook? No, he did it by having a story, mission, values, and a brand that is represented in every fun stunt he puts out there. It is ALL creativity. Don't settle for being less than awesome in how you put yourself out there. Most importantly, make it fun. If it's not fun, then you are missing the point.

ROGUE FINANCES

I am always surprised when I ask an artist how much money they need to make on average, and I am met with utter confusion. It is paramount that you understand your finances if you plan on surviving as an artist. I cover our calculations and the way we figure out our finances in The Rogue Artist's Money Guide.

One of these calculations is called "Our Weekly Money Goal." which isn't very unique, so for the sake of this book, we will call it "Rogue Average Income Needed" or making it RAIN! for short.

Weekly Rogue Budget — 2-12-2001

	A NAME	B AMOUNT	INSTRUCTIONS	C CALCULATE
WEEKLY/BI-M	BOOTH FEE	$25	WEEKLY EXPENSES: List them here.	$25
	SHOW FEE (BI-MONTHLY)	$40/2 = 20	BI-MONTHLY EXPENSES: Divide them by 2.	$20
				$45
MONTHLY	RENT	$500	MONTHLY EXPENSES: Divide them by 4.	$500
	SUBSCRIPTIONS	$15		$15
	UTILITIES	$300	UTILITIES: Add up your total utilities for the year and divide that by 12, then divide them by 4.	$300
				$815/4 = $204.00
YEARLY-QUARTERLY-BI-A	BI-INSURANCE	$405/6 =$67.5	YEARLY EXPENSES: Divide by 12, then divide by 4 weeks.	$68
	WEBSITE STUFF	$300/12 =$25	QUARTERLY: Divide by 3, then divide by 4 weeks.	$25
			BI-ANNUAL: Divide by 6, then divide by 4 weeks.	$93/4 = $24.00
BUFFER	CAR STUFF	$500/12 =$67.5	VEHICLE & MAINTENANCE	$68
	FOOD (monthly)	$172	FOOD & ENTERTAINMENT	$172
	RAINY DAY FUND	$2680/12 =$224	RAINY DAY FUND	$224
				$464/4 =$116.00
TOTAL			TOTAL WEEKLY BUDGET	$389

You can find the calculation for this in the chapter titled: IS ENOUGH GOING TO BE ENOUGH?

Weekly Rogue Budget

_____ DATE

	A NAME	B AMOUNT	INSTRUCTIONS	C CALCULATE
WEEKLY/BI-M			**WEEKLY EXPENSES:** List them here. **BI-MONTHLY EXPENSES:** Divide them by 2.	
MONTHLY			**MONTHLY EXPENSES:** Divide them by 4. **UTILITIES:** Add up your total utilities for the year and divide that by 12, then divide them by 4.	
YEARLY-QUARTERLY-BI-A			**YEARLY EXPENSES:** Divide by 12, then divide by 4 weeks. **QUARTERLY:** Divide by 3, then divide by 4 weeks. **BI-ANNUAL:** Divide by 6, then divide by 4 weeks.	
BUFFER			**VEHICLE & MAINTENANCE** **FOOD & ENTERTAINMENT** **RAINY DAY FUND** Calculate Yearly, divide by 12, then divide by 4.	
TOTAL			TOTAL WEEKLY BUDGET	

JOURNAL

Here's a second one just in case you need it.

Weekly Rogue Budget _____
DATE

	A NAME	B AMOUNT	INSTRUCTIONS	C CALCULATE
WEEKLY/BI-M			**WEEKLY EXPENSES:** List them here. **BI-MONTHLY EXPENSES:** Divide them by 2.	
MONTHLY			**MONTHLY EXPENSES:** Divide them by 4. **UTILITIES:** Add up your total utilities for the year and divide that by 12, then divide them by 4.	
YEARLY · QUARTERLY · BI-A			**YEARLY EXPENSES:** Divide by 12, then divide by 4 weeks. **QUARTERLY:** Divide by 3, then divide by 4 weeks. **BI-ANNUAL:** Divide by 6, then divide by 4 weeks.	
BUFFER			**VEHICLE & MAINTENANCE** **FOOD & ENTERTAINMENT** **RAINY DAY FUND** Calculate Yearly, divide by 12, then divide by 4.	
TOTAL			**TOTAL WEEKLY BUDGET**	

JOURNAL

Ok, here are a few more just in case.

Weekly Rogue Budget _____

DATE

	A NAME	B AMOUNT	INSTRUCTIONS	C CALCULATE
WEEKLY/BI-M			**WEEKLY EXPENSES:** List them here. **BI-MONTHLY EXPENSES:** Divide them by 2.	
MONTHLY			**MONTHLY EXPENSES:** Divide them by 4. **UTILITIES:** Add up your total utilities for the year and divide that by 12, then divide them by 4.	
YEARLY - QUARTERLY - BI-A			**YEARLY EXPENSES:** Divide by 12, then divide by 4 weeks. **QUARTERLY:** Divide by 3, then divide by 4 weeks. **BI-ANNUAL:** Divide by 6, then divide by 4 weeks.	
BUFFER			**VEHICLE & MAINTENANCE** **FOOD & ENTERTAINMENT** **RAINY DAY FUND** Calculate Yearly, divide by 12, then divide by 4.	
TOTAL			TOTAL WEEKLY BUDGET	

THE ROGUE ARTIST'S

Weekly Rogue Budget

DATE _____

	A NAME	B AMOUNT	INSTRUCTIONS	C CALCULATE
WEEKLY/BI-M			**WEEKLY EXPENSES:** List them here. **BI-MONTHLY EXPENSES:** Divide them by 2.	
MONTHLY			**MONTHLY EXPENSES:** Divide them by 4. **UTILITIES:** Add up your total utilities for the year and divide that by 12, then divide them by 4.	
YEARLY-QUARTERLY-BI-A			**YEARLY EXPENSES:** Divide by 12, then divide by 4 weeks. **QUARTERLY:** Divide by 3, then divide by 4 weeks. **BI-ANNUAL:** Divide by 6, then divide by 4 weeks.	
BUFFER			**VEHICLE & MAINTENANCE** **FOOD & ENTERTAINMENT** **RAINY DAY FUND** Calculate Yearly, divide by 12, then divide by 4.	
TOTAL			TOTAL WEEKLY BUDGET	

Weekly Rogue Budget _____

DATE

	A NAME	B AMOUNT	INSTRUCTIONS	C CALCULATE
WEEKLY/BI-M			**WEEKLY EXPENSES:** List them here. **BI-MONTHLY EXPENSES:** Divide them by 2.	
MONTHLY			**MONTHLY EXPENSES:** Divide them by 4. **UTILITIES:** Add up your total utilities for the year and divide that by 12, then divide them by 4.	
YEARLY-QUARTERLY-BI-A			**YEARLY EXPENSES:** Divide by 12, then divide by 4 weeks. **QUARTERLY:** Divide by 3, then divide by 4 weeks. **BI-ANNUAL:** Divide by 6, then divide by 4 weeks.	
BUFFER			**VEHICLE & MAINTENANCE** **FOOD & ENTERTAINMENT** **RAINY DAY FUND** Calculate Yearly, divide by 12, then divide by 4.	
TOTAL			TOTAL WEEKLY BUDGET	

MORE THAN ONE ACCOUNT

We have 3 checking accounts and 2 savings accounts with the same bank. The reason for this is managing our money and buffer money. It is a system that we came up with that helps us plan for those months that are slow. This information can be found in The Rogue Artist's Money Guide in the chapter titled "**OUR FINANCIAL ECOSYSTEM.**"

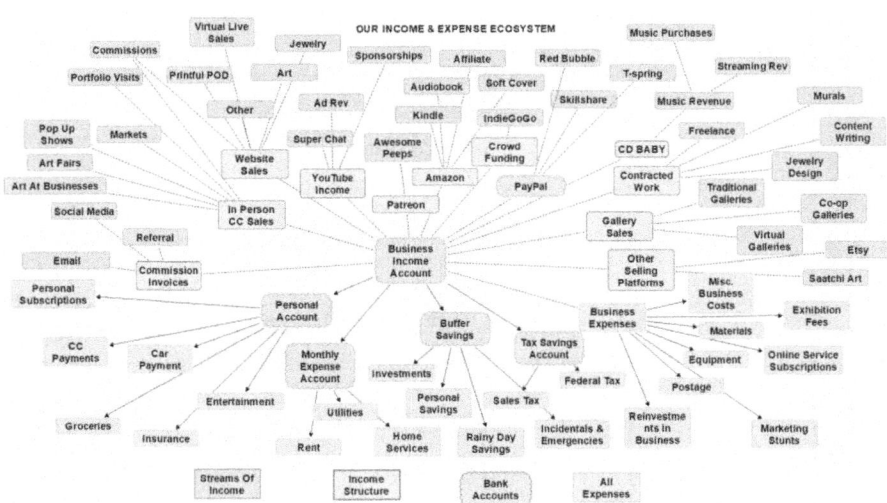

One checking account is connected to all of our creative income streams. All the money we make goes into that one account. Whether it is the sale of this book, art sold on our website, or an in-person credit card sale, it all filters into what we call our **"Business Account."**

We pay for materials, supplies, show fees, website stuff, and anything else that we need for running the business side of what we do *directly* from the business account. That makes it easy for us to see how the business is doing and also report income/expenses at tax time, because nothing non-business related happens in this account.

Anything that you pull out of your business account for use in non-business accounts are called "Personal Draws".

Our **"Personal" checking account** is where we will transfer money for food, entertainment, clothing, car payments, and other personal stuff.

Our **"House" checking account** is where we transfer the money to keep our house in order. Things like rent, utilities, and home maintenance are covered by this account.

Our **"Buffer" savings account** is where we transfer the money for our rainy day buffer and any other savings that we have.

Our **"Taxes And Business"** savings account is where we transfer the sales tax we collect, the federal taxes we calculate, and business buffer savings. When we are ready to make our tax payments, this money is transferred back into the business checking account.

The only account we use for personal spending is our personal checking. Everything else is untouchable. This keeps us from being idiots with our money.

Every week we transfer our totals, check our accounts to make sure there are no suspicious charges.

Klee keeps a ledger where she keeps track of what we can actually spend on materials from the business account. In the ledger, she subtracts the business expenses from the totals for the week, and whatever is left is ours to spend on business stuff.

We always try to have at least 4 months' worth of income in the business account, even though we have a "buffer" if things get too tight.

KEEPING TRACK OF OUR MULLA

Klee doesn't like spreadsheets, so instead of quickbooks, she uses "notebooks." She fills out the ledger while looking at the online account record to make sure everything adds up. This usually takes her around 10 minutes a day, as long as she keeps up with it.

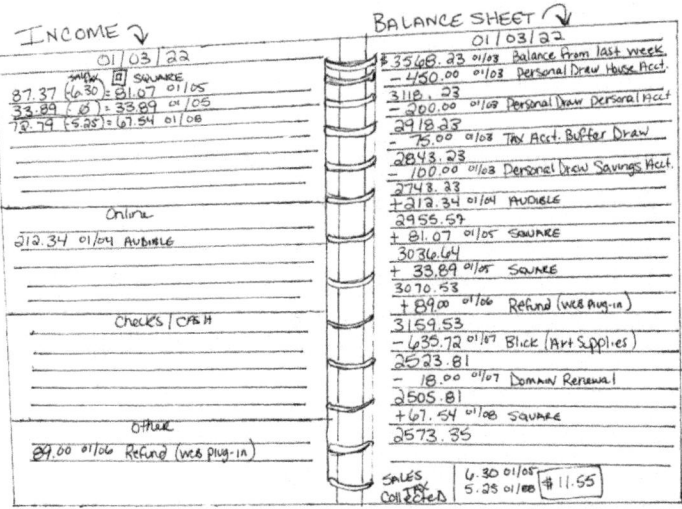

Step 1 Take whatever total you have in your business account from last week (or your current balance if you're just starting) and transfer it over to the new week (or your first week if this is a new thing). For Klee, that just means a brand new page in the notebook.

Step 2 Add any new income that flows in (credits), to that total and subtract any expenses (debits) from that total each day, updating your balance on each transaction line. This should be updated daily to make sure you don't fall behind.

Step 3 At the beginning or end of each week (you pick what works, Klee does this every Monday) transfer the amounts needed for your personal expenses (the other accounts we talked about) and record those as debits or "personal draws" in the ledger.

JOURNAL

Step 4 Check your math to make sure the numbers in your ledger match what the bank account says it has (but take into account that pending transactions may throw it off a bit until they post.)

Klee also likes to keep little notes alongside the entered income or expense that shows what date it happened and the source it's coming from or going to for reference. We have spent many times trying to figure out where a phantom number came from, so we recommend you keep at least semi-detailed notes. You can use any notebook for this, but to get you started here are a few pages to make mistakes on.

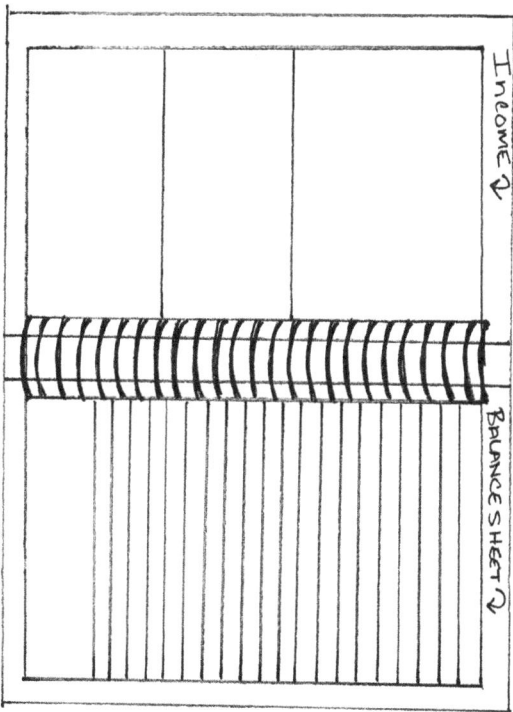

THE ROGUE ARTIST'S

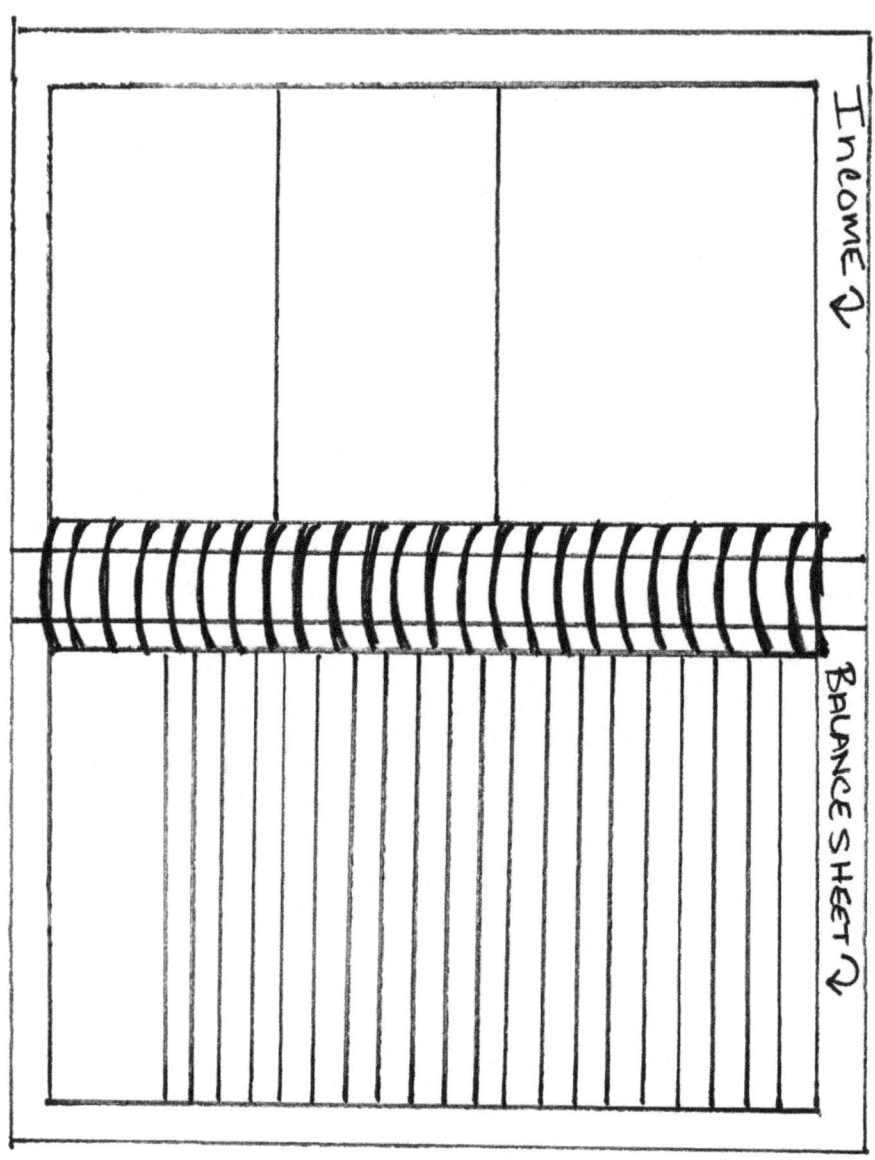

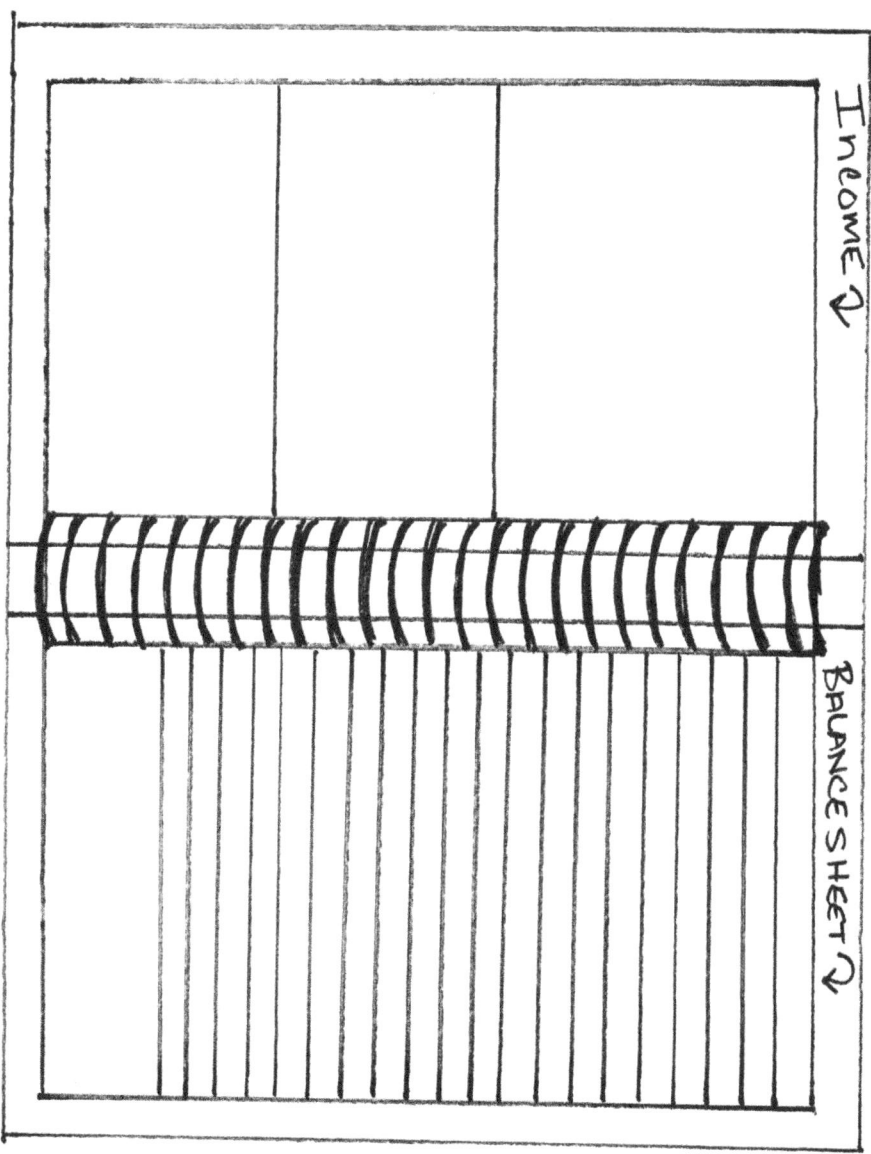

THE ROGUE ARTIST'S

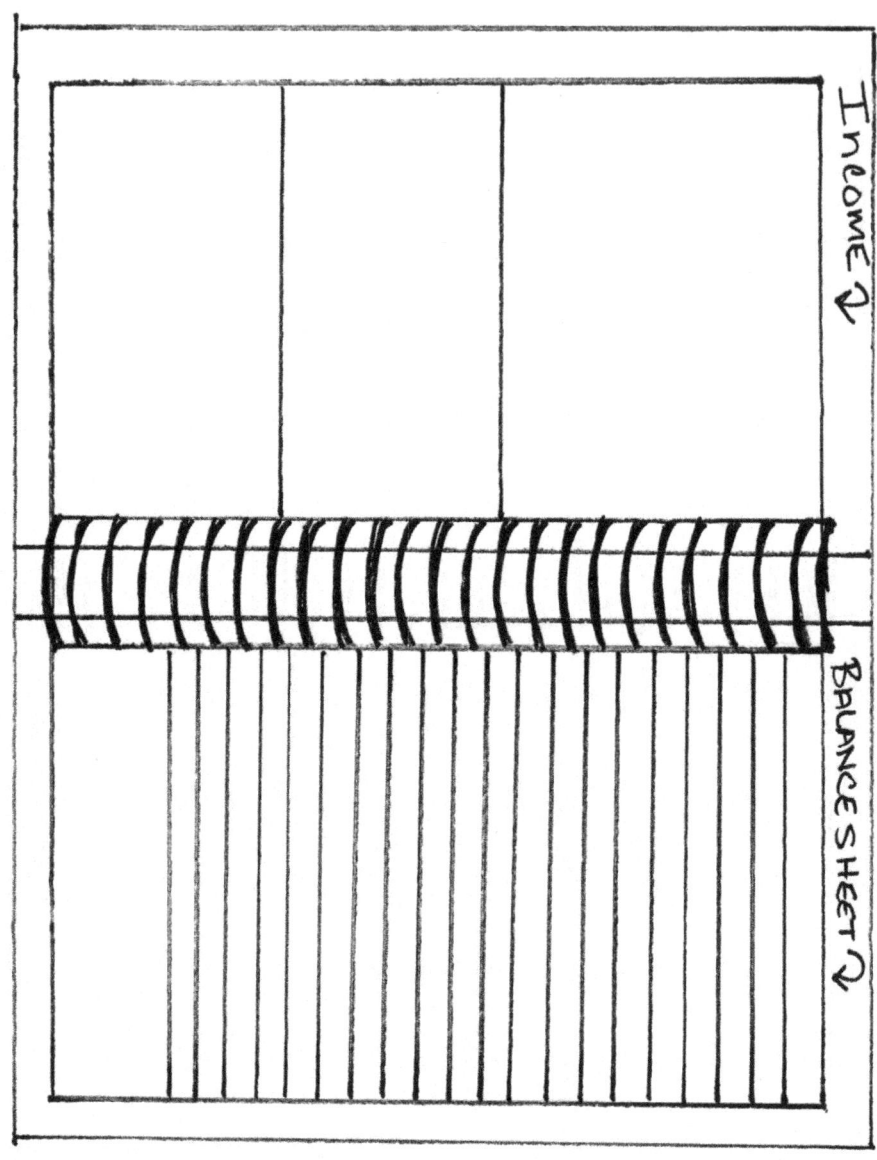

JOURNAL

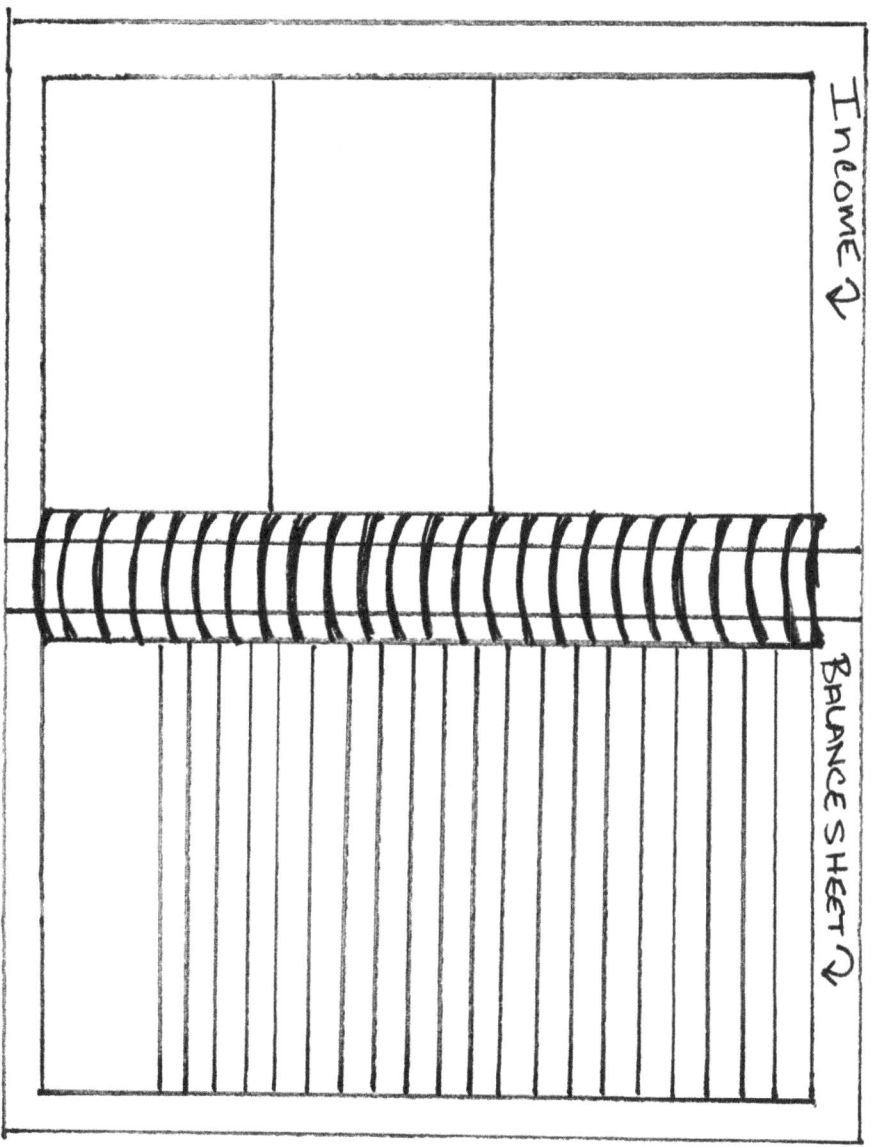

109

THE ROGUE ARTIST'S

BLOCK SCHEDULING

Klee and I use a block schedule to organize our days in the studio. I use the block schedule to give me a visual of how I can lay out my day. Many times, the concept of time is so abstract that we lose sight of how many hours we actually have available to us. There is an example of my Block schedule on the left of my media schedule board.

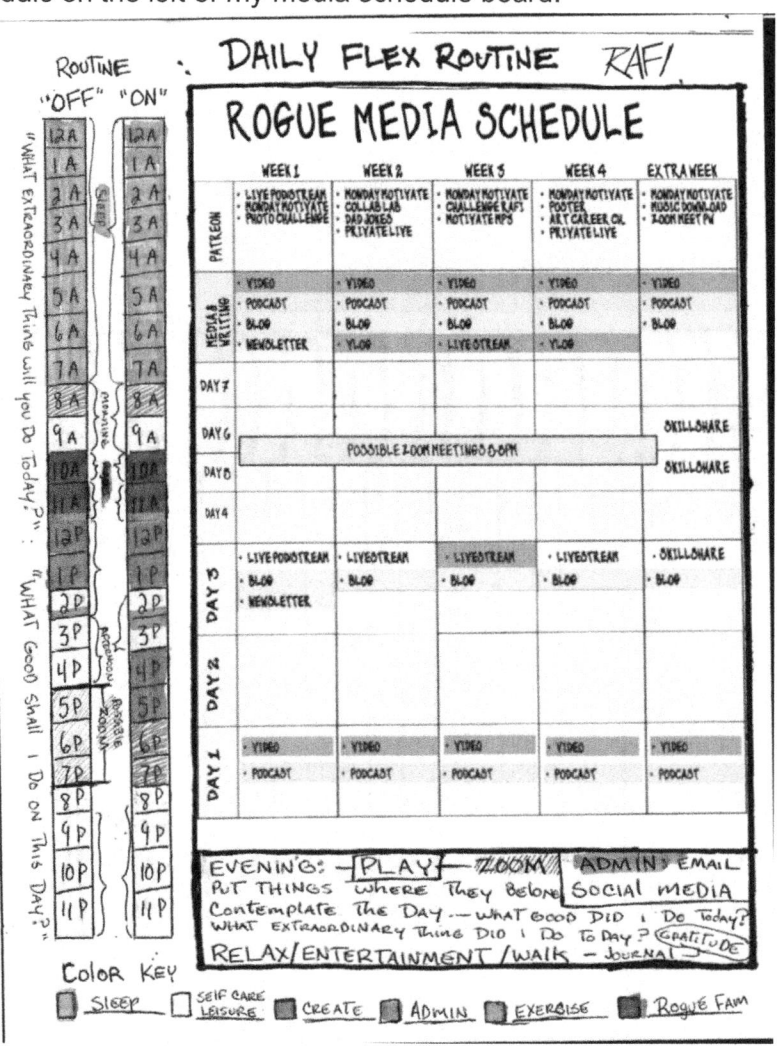

BLOCK SCHEDULE WORKSHEET

Use the empty block schedules to work out how best to utilize your time. Take into account sleep, relaxation, creation, work, exercise, admin work, and self-care. Here are a few of them. Play around with your time and see how you are using it.

THE ROGUE ARTIST'S

12A	12A	12A	12A	12A	12A
1A	1A	1A	1A	1A	1A
2A	2A	2A	2A	2A	2A
3A	3A	3A	3A	3A	3A
4A	4A	4A	4A	4A	4A
5A	5A	5A	5A	5A	5A
6A	6A	6A	6A	6A	6A
7A	7A	7A	7A	7A	7A
8A	8A	8A	8A	8A	8A
9A	9A	9A	9A	9A	9A
10A	10A	10A	10A	10A	10A
11A	11A	11A	11A	11A	11A
12P	12P	12P	12P	12P	12P
1P	1P	1P	1P	1P	1P
2P	2P	2P	2P	2P	2P
3P	3P	3P	3P	3P	3P
4P	4P	4P	4P	4P	4P
5P	5P	5P	5P	5P	5P
6P	6P	6P	6P	6P	6P
7P	7P	7P	7P	7P	7P
8P	8P	8P	8P	8P	8P
9P	9P	9P	9P	9P	9P
10P	10P	10P	10P	10P	10P
11P	11P	11P	11P	11P	11P

JOURNAL

Am I spending my time in the best way possible?

Could I spend my time better?

Do I value my time? More than money? Which is finite?
Obviously, you know how I feel about this subject because I wrote an entire section about it in my money book. However, I want you to investigate it for yourself.

MONTHLY MEDIA SCHEDULE

If you are planning on doing videos, podcasts, blogs, or anything else online it is ideal to give yourself a consistent schedule. You want to make sure that it is sustainable for you, since you need time to work on your art and don't want to spend all your time online. I have mine broken into time increments. I work on media stuff for about one to two hours a day.

I have one media day where I spend the day editing videos, podcasts because those will be the most time consuming. Again, make sure you are not putting too much on your plate because you will burn out. This schedule is an example of too much, so take this and cut it in half. I am currently in the process of reworking it.

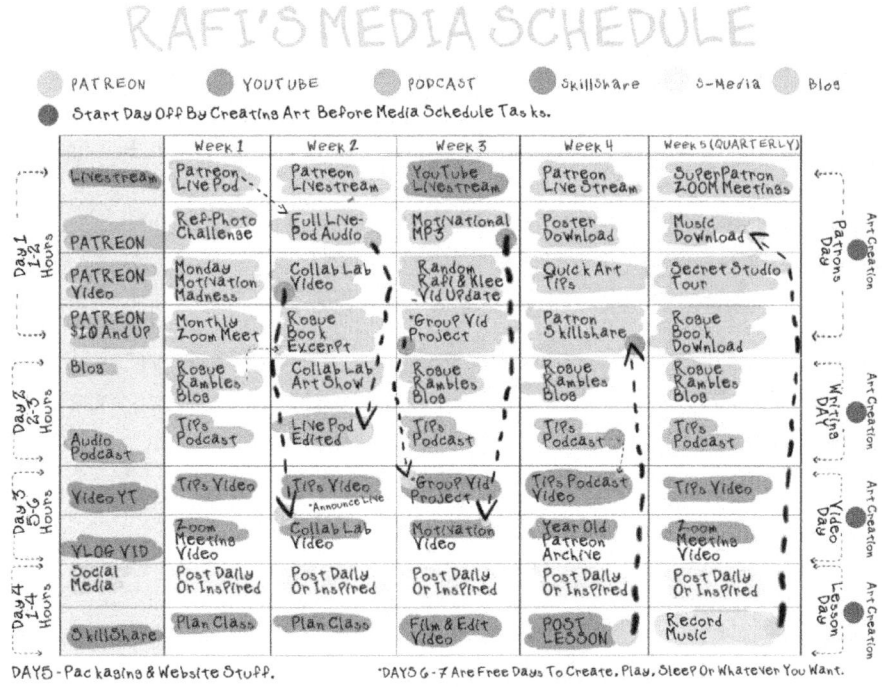

I have my months broken down to 4 weeks, and every quarter there is an extra week (5th week).

Whenever I do any quarterly events or virtual sales, it will usually land on the extra week. Most weekly planners have the same layout. This media schedule allows me to look at a week and determine what needs to get done. Again, don't give yourself too much, this schedule is ridiculous. I recommend a max of 2 - 3 media obligations (not including social media posts) like videos or podcasts. Even then, you can cut that down to monthly or bi-monthly if need be. Make it comfortable for you.

Either way, just remember that this will constantly be changing and it will be in flux. Use scheduling to help you make sense of your time but don't become a slave to your schedule.

MONTHLY MEDIA SCHEDULE WORKSHEET

See if you could put together a media schedule that works for you. I've added a few of these, so don't be afraid to mess it up.

Week	MONTHLY MEDIA SCHEDULE								
	M	T	W	T	F	S	S	Weekly To Do	
1									
2									
3									
4									
Extra									
Daily To do								Notes And Monthly Message	
Day Primary									
Day Secondary									

Week	M	T	W	T	F	S	S	Weekly To Do
1								
2								
3								
4								
Extra								
Daily To do								Notes And Monthly Message
Day Primary								
Day Secondary								

MONTHLY MEDIA SCHEDULE

THE ROGUE ARTIST'S

Week	M	T	W	T	F	S	S	Weekly To Do
1								
2								
3								
4								
Extra								
Daily To do								Notes And Monthly Message
Day Primary								
Day Secondary								

MONTHLY MEDIA SCHEDULE

Week	M	T	W	MONTHLY MEDIA SCHEDULE T	F	S	S	Weekly To Do
1								
2								
3								
4								
Extra								
Daily To do					Notes And Monthly Message			
Day Primary								
Day Secondary								

WEEKLY BUSINESS SCHEDULE

The following pages have a layout of what I do in my weekly planner. It has a page to list events, deadlines, meetings, and stuff you have going on throughout the week. The other page will have your Fan-4-List and financial tracking section.

The Fan-4-List
I have gotten in the habit of using something I call a Fantastic 4 List. These are 4 important things that I want to get done sooner than later. The things on this list could be as simple as sending an email, making a phone call, or putting a layer on a painting. It just needs to be significant to grow in your art career. Having a Fantastic 4 List allows you to continually keep track of the things that you want to reach. Instead of tackling a large overwhelming project all at once, it enables you to break it down into smaller, manageable chunks. List four things you want to get done that week. Once you finish something, cross it off and move to the next item. Every day that week make sure you add an item to the bottom of the list whenever you cross something off. Use this for ongoing and large projects that you have running in the background of your day. If you have items left at the end of the week, transfer them over to the next week.

Financial Tracking.
It is important to know your finances and to check it often. Every week put your balance in and write down all of your expenses and deposits. Also keep track of what you have in your buffer accounts.

Week Numbers
Each week has a number that correlates with your Monthly Media Schedule so you can add what is appropriate for the week. The first two months in each quarter will have 4 weeks and the third month will have 5 weeks. Usually when I have a quarterly event, this is the week it gets scheduled since technically it is an extra week in the quarter.

Room Around the Planner
I use this room around the planner for additional notes and anything else I may need.

Write down in the space below what your perfect day would look like. Then aim to make that a reality.

WEEK 1   MONTH _____

MONDAY	
TUESDAY	
WEDNESDAY	
THURSDAY		SATURDAY	
FRIDAY		SUNDAY	

FAN-4-LIST

_____
_____
_____
_____
_____
_____
_____
_____
_____
_____

	BUFFER & HOUSE Accounts		
RAINY D	HOUSE & CAR	TAX BUFFER	

FINANCIALS

	AMOUNT
BALANCE	
TRANSFERS & EXPENSES	
DEPOSITS (– TAX collected)	
END BALANCE	

MAXIMIZE YOUR PROFITS

In building your creative empire, you want to think of all the different ways you can make money with your creativity. The best way to do this is to think of your multiple streams of income.

As an artist, I may create a painting that takes me several days to finish. Once the piece is done, I will list it for sale on my website for $800.

My potential income would be limited to the sale of that work of art, and when it is gone, it is gone.

How else can you make money on the image? Can it become a:

- **T-shirt or clothing.** I will sometimes edit the image, use only specific elements in the painting, add some text, and make it work for a cool t-shirt or clothing design.
- **Postcards or holiday cards.** I will create special postcards or holiday cards with fun sayings.
- **Calendars.** Every year, I will pick some of the art I create for inclusion in my yearly calendar.
- **Poster And Prints.** I create posters with my artist logo and photo prints which are done through a POD site through my website.
- **Home goods.** I'll design mugs and other items like iPhone cases and pillows.
- **Digital works.** This is a printable print of my work, or a screensaver.
- **Stickers**. Stickers of my work and small knick knacks.
- **NTFs.** At the time of the release of this book, this is a relatively new market, but may become a digital standard in the future.

These are just some examples of how you can maximize your profits. Go a little further and see what you can do with other talents.

- Getting A Part-Time Job
- Taking On Freelancing Gigs
- Affiliate Programs For Things You Use.
- Sell Original Works
- Commissions
- Sell Prints Or Reproductions Of Your Work
- Sell Print-On-Demand Products
- Offer Freelance Art Services
- Sell Commercial Licenses For Your Digital Art
- Lease Your Art
- Do Graphic Design
- Design Custom Fonts
- Design Logos
- Create Procreate Brushes
- Create Illustrator & Photoshop Brushes
- Music Editing
- Listing Your Spare Space On Airbnb
- Make Money In Rental Income
- Collaborate With Businesses
- Teach One On One Art Lessons
- Teach Art Workshops
- Teach A Class On A Learning Platform
- Start A Patreon
- Start A Blog
- Start A Artist Vlog On Youtube
- Sell On Social Media
- Do The Art Festival Circuit
- Do Small Art Shows
- Do Farmers Markets
- Sell Digital Downloadable Pdfs Of Your Art
- Sell Digital Graphics Of Your Art
- Tour With Music
- Producing Music For Other Musicians
- Produce Music
- Play Music Gigs
- Upload Your Music For Distribution
- Teach Music
- Write A Book And Self Publish
- Get Paid To Write Articles
- Copywriting
- Writing Courses
- Record Audio Books
- Podcasting
- Announcements
- Make Invitations
- Make Greeting Cards
- Make Wine Labels
- Make Calendars
- Make Stickers
- Make Mugs
- Make Posters
- Make Bags
- Create And Sell Sewing Patterns
- Photography
- Lightroom Or Photoshop Design
- Product Mockups
- Product Photography
- Video Editing
- Filming
- Jingle Writing
- Write Resumes For Others
- Voiceover Recording
- Music For Videos
- Jewelry Design
- Jewelry Repair
- Consulting Services
- And So Many More!

BRAINSTORM YOUR INCOME

Think about different things that you are already good at. How can you make some income from that? Do you have certain experience that you can offer consultations? Do you have a skill that you can monetize? Do you create anything that can become a passive income stream? Go ahead and brain dump on the following pages.

BRAINSTORM

THE ROGUE ARTIST'S

BRAINSTORM

BRAINSTORM

WRITE OR SKETCH ALL YOUR IDEAS DOWN.

Get in the habit of writing everything down, whether it is:
- An idea. Pricing calculations. Thoughts.
- Painting sketch.
- Notes for a project idea.
- Video ideas.
- Something that inspires you.
- A plan for greatness.
- A to-do list.
- Random marketing ideas.
- Some philosophy you want to research.
- A new perspective.
- Something you saw that you want to remember.
- Song, poetry, or writing ideas.
- Or just some excellent random thought you have.

Here is some extra room to do it! Hope you enjoyed our journey into the creative genius that is you. Now go out there and take the word by storm!

NOTES

NOTES

NOTES

NOTES

NOTES

NOTES

NOTES

NOTES

Made in United States
North Haven, CT
06 June 2022